David,
I hope you
enjoy this book
of my poetry
from your
loving father.
Never forget.

David,
I hope you enjoy this book

Propaganda Begins with PR

Poetry for the Soul

by

Meredith Z. Avakian

authorHOUSE®

AuthorHouse™
1663 Liberty Drive, Suite 200
Bloomington, IN 47403
www.authorhouse.com
Phone: 1-800-839-8640

First published by AuthorHouse 9/12/2008

ISBN: 978-1-4389-0832-8 (sc)

Printed in the United States of America
Bloomington, Indiana

This book is printed on acid-free paper.

About the author...

Meredith **"Miz"** Avakian is a New Jersey native of **Armenian-American** descent who has been writing **poetry** since she was a child. She received a bachelor's degree in **public relations** from Temple University and continues to reside in Philadelphia, Pa.

Although most of her work is shared through **live performances**, some of her poetry has been published in various print and online publications including the Armenian Mirror-Spectator, the Armenian Poetry Project, Poetry Ink and The Literary Groong.

She has spent most of her life searching for a sense of **justice** in the world's inequalities. The message is underlined throughout her poetry and time dedicated to volunteering for community events. Both her personal and professional lives revolve around communications and the role that **"having a voice"** plays in society

Acknowledgements...

This book is dedicated to everyone who has inspired, encouraged, motivated, supported and believed in me, especially:

My beloved grandparents, Leon S. & Ruth A. Avakian;

The Armenian community of Philadelphia; and,

Temple University's Poetry as Performance (2:40) family.

As a woman of many words, I can't seem to think of anything more powerful to say except, "Thank you. I love you."

Table of Contents

Who Am I?

Go Armo!

Politics 101

Poetry Is Not a Luxury

Love vs. Lust

2:40

Who Am I?

Blind Existence

I am the warm flesh of justice
I wonder why God chose me
I hear oppressive cries echoing in the air
I see the invisible boundaries of despair
I am the butterfly breaking from ball & chain

I pretend you'll all remember my name
I feel freedom through my veins
I touch tears flowing, let it rain, let it reign
I worry about future's fate
I am the warm flesh of justice

I understand I'm misunderstood
I say exhale the funk of inequality…for good
I dream of a better tomorrow
I try to eliminate the sorrow
I hope reincarnation continues my legacy
I am the warm flesh of justice, respect my existence

Armed & Dangerous

You said my poetry scares you
You said my poetry scares you…
So much, that you need protection
I am not surprised

In fact, take off the bulletproof vest
And wrap your cranium with Kevlar
So when I shoot piercing words through your ears
Your brain will numbingly reflect on just
How fucking deep they are

You know what?
Perhaps I should spit poems through condoms
To perform safe and protected poetry for you
I'll turn poetry into STD's
So your ears could be tested positive

And don't think a burner will protect you
Because I'll spit hot fire that'll melt the glock while it's cocked
And brand "M" in your hand like the Home Alone man

So what may I ask scares you
Is it
A- The energy, power, words or lesson?
Your comment's so vague – it keeps me guessin'
B- Does the thought of a woman expressing herself
result in a man's loss of supremacy and stealth?
C- Does my ability of honesty lead to vulnerability and insecurity?
D- Do my words of truth translate as uncouth?
If so, you know I advise you not to cover your ears
And prevent what you hear
I'll be loud and clear
And will pump you with fear

Shoot, I've always been a little nervous

about multiple choice my damn self
So if the answer's "E" - none of the above
Tell me why you don't show love

[sccch] 5-0-5-0
Be on the lookout for a Spanish-looking woman
with long, black hair
Mid to late 20s
Approximately 5'2", 130 lbs.
She's reportedly been using her freedom of speech to heat up mics
in the tri-state area
She is armed and dangerous
I repeat...armed and dangerous
Roger – over and out

That's right
In the words of Lyrispect,
"Say hello to my little pen"
Cuz "I've gotta poem and I'm not afraid to use it"
I'll spray you with the words I spit
Until your entire body's less of shit
So get the crap outta your head

I'm not angry or mad at the world or filled with rage
I'm just an educated Armenian with a voice and a stage
Who makes words come to life from a page
So I can scare you once
Or maybe twice
Depending on if I want to be
Naughty or nice
So be afraid
Be very afraid
Because I am armed and dangerous

Old Soul

Many have said I'm an old soul
Been reincarnated through centuries
Or so I'm told
It'd explain my old, excuse me, mature ways
And why I feel aged day-to-day

I've fought with the Mongolians
Leading their conquests
Was a Greek woman in another past life
Just wonder what's next
Already fought my battles
Dying way before my time
So this time around
I'm gonna make it mine

This life is my chance
Now is the time
For this mind, body & opportunity
To accomplish every possibility
So I hurry, hurry, hurry
To make up for lost time
Though I don't recall living it
My mission carries on

No wonder time's run matters so much
Haunting, following, counting
The old soul who may soon have to "cross over"
Not that the past were mistakes
Most likely preparation
Knowing how great the cause is
And how important it is to do it right

Maybe I'll stick around as long as I can
Perhaps coming back in the form of a man
Still the same drive and determination
Striving for reign – the obligation
Finally ready to lead, teach and learn
That's why I remain busy
Because this lifetime's my turn

Do I Know You?

I can't stand it when you're so critical about yourself
Sometimes quicker to judge than everyone else
You act like you're a beast
When you look in the mirror
The feeling should be deceased
Cuz deep down, I know that you know you're a beauty

I can't stand it when you interrupt me
As if I'm not even there
You don't even care
You're just thinking about you

I can't stand it when you use that tone of voice
I know it's not your choice
But I'm kinda annoyed

I can't stand it when you look at me that way
Like I'm supposed to obey
Everything you do and say

I can't stand it when you pity yourself
Knowing damn well life could be worse
And you sometimes act like you're cursed

I can't stand it when you stress
Don't you care about your health?
Please tell me why am I so critical of myself?

I Am Not My Skin

I am not my skin

My spirit lives somewhere above, beyond and below my epidermis
This almond-cream complexion is attached to something real
But like the skin of bananas
It can tend to peel

But I am not my skin

I am more than the passing privilege
that my people aren't always permitted
No survey/questionnaire/"for statistical purposes only"
can reveal my identity
Not the snow white, flake, cracker
Nor sand-nigger, spick
Which I've all been called
You see, these words don't define me at all

Because I am not my skin

True, my external's created experiences
based on the vision of others
But to exist as semi-deceased
Doesn't differ from another
Sun block can't hide it
Suntan can't disguise it
Sun mist can't make it
Because it's here year round
The specialty that makes me me
Is found much further down

Therefore, I am not my skin

Not the stereotype that you'd like
Depending on the season
Though thick and tough
It's not enough
Please give another reason
To know who I am before I speak
Or care to stare
Like I don't know you're there
But "Somebody's watchin' me"

I am not my skin

My spirit existed before my body, wrinkles, freckles and hair
But too many people cover up
The me I like to wear
Those trapped in the illusion
That a tone or two or three
Is what's making me me
Should reevaluate themselves
Because to judge is sin
And what lies within the skin is melanin
So let's begin
Closing our eyes
And opening our minds

My Favorite Things

Dolma and kufta, macaroni & cheese
Pizza and subs, Middle Eastern, Chinese
Hibachi and fondue are alright with me
These are a few of my favorite things

Barbecue chicken, watermelon, iced tea
Pickles, honey turkey, French fries, onion strings
Armenian, Brazilian, Mexican cuisine
These are a few of my favorite things

When my stomach growls
When I salivate
When I'm feeling hungry
I simply remember my favorite things
And I then I go out to eat

Thank You

Thanks for making me beautiful
My words of praise cannot lift you higher than you are
Reflections of strength break chains of weak ignorance
Fierce cheek bones curve to unite justice
Compliment brown eye gazing back into the darkness

Thank you for the darkness
The polyrhythmic beats that intertwine to create culture
And memories that trace back to past lives
The deep mahogany features that question the average
Into what exotic stance is taken, given by you
You who deliver my presence and dictate my life subconsciously
Through your visions whispered to me in my dreams

Thank you for the dreams
The hope that comes with them
The untold stories my nightly senses distribute
The puzzle pieces that fit somewhere in this life
The solutions that need to be figured out
Wishing, yearning and dissolving as the sun rises

Thank you for your nourishment
For the song and dance that guide my heart
For feeding my soul with your wealth's richness
The kind of nourishment that leaves me full
With just the thought of devouring it

Thank you

Go Armo!

1915

Call me genocide
Call me rape
Call me extermination
Call me slaughter
Call me massacre
But never call me a lie

The systemized, strategized murder of masses
to a particular demographic
The havoc, the elimination, extermination planned to a nation
The concentration camps…before Jews were stamped
My people were cramped into mass burial graves
We were not born as slaves
Yet forced to behave by means to obey
A God that's not ours and give our bodies for free
And by give I mean take
Because there's nothing consensual about cold-blooded rape
Followed by slaughter of mothers and daughters
While the heads of men became trophies and sat on sticks
Till all the blood drained out…it's straight sick
As if that's not enough they were put on display
As a lesson to obey
But the damage was done before we could run
Because we were forced to march until the end was the start
And the start was the end
Starved. Hung. Shot. Stabbed. Dehydrated.
Just to name a few of the obstacles to die through
Antagonized. Sodomized. Ridiculed and more
How dare they call it a war!

Call me genocide
Call me rape
Call me extermination
Call me slaughter
Call me massacre
But NEVER call me a lie!

Picking Up the Pieces (The Vase)

Some call it a vāse & some call it a văse
I alternate depending on what mood I'm in
I'll choose to say vase today
But regardless, it's symbolic of a people
A great people that were displaced
Like the pieces of this broken vase

Scattered & distorted
Picked up & aborted
Moved & confused
But they remain the same
Different pieces of the same vase
Many linking to one
One land. One nation. One people.
One greater whole.
That we'll never know
But understand that it once was
It once was
It once was
And always will be
One beautiful vase

I am a piece of this broken vase
I may not look the same as the others
But the whole is incomplete without me
My matter is tattered
But that doesn't matter
Because I am no less than the bigger pieces
Nor larger than those
Whole colors are exposed
And fit the unity of the once believed identity
From which eternity birthed infinity
Which calculates as the sum that I'll never know

Pick up the pieces
I challenge you to find one
From the same mold – young or old
That you'll recognize as an equal...
Contribution without exclusion
Considered a mere sequel
Embrace the difference
And recognize the similarities
You're part of the same vase

Yes, it may've been broken
Beaten, hidden & damaged
Some were lost along the way
And others seemed to manage
It's not complete
Without unity
How can we recreate?
But if you constantly search
And pick up the pieces
One at a time
And keep them together
Bound by need
You'll gather the remains and be amazed
When you start to see
What are still the makings of
One beautiful vase.

Hayastan

During my many years,
I've been called many names
Persian, Roman, Ottoman, Babylonian, Byzantine
I mean, the list goes on
Most call me Turkey now,
But the hundreds and hundreds of thousands of natives
whose blood has saturated my roots know that's a bunch of gobble
As their souls still can be felt in the wind,
Their spirits are mounted at the top of Masis,
And the beats of their hearts ripple across Lake Van

Yes, I've had many names and my placement changes just the same
They keep pushing
They keep pushing me
And dammit one day I will take back the map
To give my latitude & longitude the geographic respect it deserves
What do I look like?
What is a land without its people?
How dare I be called out of my rightful name
I shall exist as long as I believe lives weren't lost in vain
And the pain is insane
Because it's felt around the world

Come back to me
Bring me your blessings
So I can be called home again
For those who know that I'm more than lakes & trees
& mountains & grass
I ask...find your way
True, I've been a land of many names,
but those who knew me at my best,
Will always remember me as Hayastan

Armenian Queen

Mother from Egypt
Father from Turkey
Well, the land formerly known as Armenia
Bearing the same blood from both
All with large noses and ethnic features
Daughter of immigrants
She grew up in a two-bedroom apartment in Jersey City
Where her parents sheltered her
From poverty and tragedy
Yet, still no stranger to hard work
She grew up hearing what it was like back home
Far from the streets of Jersey
Where the blood of many relatives tragically stained the soil
To be left in her roots
And those of her husband
Whose orphan mother and dark-skinned father
Knew all too well
They managed to make it to the States
As they had to escape the fate
That three young men brought to millions
In a new place, the couple assimilates
Losing the language almost as quickly as family
Surviving by means of conformity
To some degree
But for a better life
This wife
Never forgot the memories
Never forgot the recipes
Never forgot the families
And birthed two sons
Who knew of the tragedies
But were too distant to relate
To lost relatives
Too far to understand
Too few who knew

So she grew…into grandmotherhood
With four legacies to be specific
Knowing she must pass the torch
As it'd once been handed down to her
Fueled by the internal flame
That her relatives were burned for having
Mother from Egypt
Father from Turkey
Born in America
Still an Armenian Queen
And I call her Grams

My Life as an Armenian

With features this dark
And hair this thick
People get confused
On what ethnicity to pick
It matters so much for some…
…to know if I'm one of them
But I am one of none
Even if they let me in
A never-ending search for identity is how we're born
Torn, from everything we knew, owned, loved and cherished
It all perished

But my life as an Armenian
Has made me proud
I'll scream it aloud
In front of a Turkish crowd

I'll need for you to understand
That when any man
Asks "what" I am
It's not a one-word answer
I'll preach to you
And won't be through
You'll want me gone like cancer

My life as an Armenian
Has led me to check off "other"
On the race portion of surveys
And write down "human" on the line
Not everyone can fit into one of those damn little boxes
So we assimilate and concentrate
On where we'd best be accepted
But it aggravates and frustrates
Those who'll be neglected and rejected

My life as an Armenian
Has led me to get excited
When I see "ian" at the end of a last name
It feels like finding lost family
Or understanding just the same

My life as an Armenian
Has led me to take out the white in the American flag
Replacing it with orange
Still keeping the blue and the red
That's for the sky and bloodshed
Since the majority of my people are dead
Died of the "forgotten genocide"
So the memory I hope to keep alive
They question me so much
They've got me questioning myself
Wondering why they think pork is so good for my health
Unique and alone
Critique the word home
Mystique of the roam

My life as an Armenian
Makes me wonder why I don't just say I'm American
But Amer-I-can't
We have names most can't pronounce
Food that some denounce
And passion with every pounce
I grew up a mere minnow
Lost in a sea of Aryan sharks
Then it all flipped
Like, "Go back to start."
I'm tired of defending who I am
And where I'm from
But it apparently matters to everyone
So know that the Middle East is not to be confused with Europe
And if European equals "white"
You do the math, alright?

I Will Not Forget

Don't worry, I will not forget
I always will remember the stories you've shared
Even the ones that hurt to think about
Including how your father had his head split open just for running
into the Turkish children on the way to school one morning
Yes, the past is the past, but I will not forget it

Grandma, don't you worry, I will never forget your cooking
It's what always kept the family together,
and I promise to keep us bound after you're gone
No one can cook dolma quite like you, but I will try to remember
your recipes as they've been passed down to me

I know that your grandparents lived every day
wishing they could forget
But if they died knowing that I would remember
I think they would be proud
So not only will I serve as a symbol of remembrance,
But I will share their experiences aloud

You know you don't have to worry
I will not forget the work that was put in
just to make sure I succeed
Your assimilation and conformity may not be to my liking,
But I recognize that it was done for me
At the end of the day, you have not forgotten where you come from
And you know that I will not forget

Rest assured that in decades that last
This feeling won't pass
The notion of hope and remembrance
Your generation has fought its battles
Now it is time for us to finish this war
Excuse me; I will not forget that it never was a war
I will remember it as genocide, don't you worry

Grandma, I could never forget you
As I see my smile in yours and yours in your mothers
I'm sure my children will resemble the same
You know that everything about you will be remembered
And your parents would be proud to know that you never forgot
When you see them, please let them know
I will never forget

First for Everything

I wanted to laugh
I wanted to cry
I did cry
But I wanted to laugh

Still, tears streamed…
…uncontrollably for a second
But then I chuckled
My first Armenian Church service

So emotional
Didn't have to understand the words to feel the energy…
The sadness…
The mourning…
The tears

Then, the attire caused a smirk
The cloaks, the hoods, the collars
It's really quite comical if you're not used to it
The giggles

Foreign among foreigners
"I feel like I stand out"
But they looked like me
Still, I was not one
Not then

For as long as they chant,
I will laugh
And as long as the incense burns,
I will cry
Giggles and tears

My first Armenian Church service
Certainly won't be my last

Politics 101

Origins (God Bless America Piece)

God Bless America!

I live in a country
Where the red, white and blue
Have nothing to do
With liberty and justice for all
Justice is just ice
Lasting one trillionth of a second in hell
And I tell…you that the blue reps the blues
Cried by the oppressed
The red is for the bloodshed
And I stress
The white stands for the so-called "dominant race"
Though the average color of face
Tends to be
A little more toward ebony
And I'm surprised they're letting me
Use my freedom of speech
Should I be speared?
Cuz, "Oops, I did it again!"
Running my mouth about the truth
But I'm going to heaven
Since "In God I Trust"
Say it if I must

God Bless America!

This god-less America
Was built on hysteria
Re-founded by murder and genocide
I wish Columbus had died
Before his mom shit him out
And the fact that he's honored
Makes me want to shout

God Bless America!

The 11th of September
Made me remember
Why everyone hates the States
And I debate
My status in pride
It's like mental masturbation
Because I'm screwing with my head
If it weren't for America,
My family probably would be dead
But as we survived our genocide
Others strived to stay alive
Leading my thoughts astray
And causing me to say

God Bless America!

My country 'tis of thee
Sweet land of hypocrisy
To thee I think
Why cover my heart with my hand
And pledge allegiance
To something I don't believe?
It's not that I don't understand
I just can't conceive
My indifference toward my nation
Since its origins were not God's creation
I never argued before today
I just went along and would say

God Bless America!

This melting pot's
Really a crock
Of boiling bullshit
Where a region of this country salutes the wrong flag
I wouldn't even use it as a rag
I don't mean to nag
Fuck that! Yes, I do.
The South should realize that slavery is supposed to be through
The Confederate flag doesn't shout "Southern pride"
It shouts "Slavery's alive!"
And I shout

God Bless America!

The land of opportunity
For whom?
Don't get me started on how open the door is
For immigrants to come through
And the 4ᵗʰ of July
Is just an excuse
For everyone to get drunk and act a fool
As they watch fireworks by a pool
Might I add the White House was properly named
There's no coincidental pattern
To who's been famed
This isn't the land of the free
And home of the brave
It's the land where we bleed
And home of the slaves

God Bless America!

God Bless America?

God, bless America.

National Insecurity

I was raped
Couldn't escape
Held down by a man
Named Uncle Sam
And taken advantage of
He saw that I have no bush
Like we have no president
I tried so hard to push
But on and on he went
My ears were forced to hear
As he screamed "I want you!"
"I want you!!"
"I want you!!!"
But my body will not be a statistic
Of how we supposedly fight for peace
Though I was imperially invaded
And beat with bureaucracy
I couldn't get him off of me
I am a victim
Of the judicial system
And even if I die twice
And am born again for a third time
I still wouldn't be a virgin
Because I was raped at birth
He stripped me before I could see
My rights, expectations and dignity
I tried to hide
But the only thing on my side
Was American pride
In which I could not confide
Because he told me we're all equal...
...but he lied
Help!
He captured me with capitalism
Someone rescue me!

All the Robin Hoods
Are white-collared, too busy out robbin' hoods
He was given a dick to restrict
I was retrained to feel the pain
At that time
He had a mental muzzle on my mind
And that's fine
For most of you
But I chose to break through
What's my excuse?
Freedom, perhaps
In fact, perhaps freedom is the reason for treason
Before he began to stick it in
That crook made me look
And said, "This is bigger and better than any other"
Before I could discover from another
I was raped undercover
Not under covers
He didn't manage to succeed
Since his seeds
Weren't planted in me
But this serial rapist has screwed all of "us" in U.S.

Broadcast This

Who the hell do you think you are?

Telling women how they should look
What they should wear, where they should buy it
And for how much,
The invaluable worth of our women,
Saddened by your lies and propaganda?
And for what, your hidden agenda?
It's not so concealed after all
And we will not stand for it
In fact, let us boycott your scheming
And all remain screaming

Who the hell do you think you are?

Telling our communities who the criminals are
Last time I checked,
the government was responsible for the lack of universal health care,
poor educational systems and loss of social security
After all, where do you think the drugs and guns came from
in the first place?
The offenses are from offices
And the puppets attached to them
Perhaps if they were forced to do their "job" on street corners
People would see things a little differently

Who the hell do you think you are?

Trying to scare us with your terrifying tactics
Don't eat this, don't shop here, don't travel there
You can't even make up your mind
whether or not we should be eating eggs
And we're supposed to trust you for our daily information?
Well guess what?
The only thing more frightening than you is your supporters

Who the hell do you think you are?

Subjectively reporting war "news"
And expecting us to shed tears and grow hatred
And you wonder why they want to translate the political debates
Perhaps the context already has been lost
Along with how many lives overseas?
How many lives in these streets?
You can make me try to cease,
But I will not desist!
I'll continue to resist

Who the hell do you think you are?
Because you're nothing but a joke to me.
I don't take you seriously
I just wanted to check the weather forecast on t.v.

Propaganda Begins with PR

Propaganda
PR-op-aganda
PR-op-agenda
Prop agenda
Propaganda Begins with PR

PR & Propaganda
Both accused of lying by omission
Ideas, facts, allegations
Individuals, companies, nations
Establishing and maintaining an image
Persuading others to see things one way
Spreading information
Ideas, facts, allegations
Maintaining the created images
Of people, places, things
Not to be confused with the following:
Advertising, marketing, promotions or HR

Propaganda
Before the word was created or translated
There just was no known name
But its history is longer than it's credited
It's helped to start wars,
Elect leaders into office,
Persuade the common folk to smoke
Influence people on how to live their lives
And allow establishments to do the thinking for them

PR
Similar ideology to influence and persuade
Meaning a liaison, per "say"
But should be done in a different way
Often referred to as publicity
Never to be synonymous with the terms "spin" or "flack"

Supposed to be held to highest ethical standards
And purely based on facts
Not always appears tasteful
But should be done with tact
The difference is defined
By how professionals act

Propaganda Begins with PR
And ends with "duh"
I love my job

F.U.T.U.

F.U.T.U.

For not saying you're a five-year school
Or not telling us that you're the dummies
So we all play the fool
Buying tools – like books and such
Spending a grip
(I'm talking way too much)
Using construction as your crutch
I prefer to call it a scapegoat
How you rape hope
Freshman take note
On how they make dope
These hustlers
Just out for a buck
Raping anyone they care to fuck
Well, it's not just anyone nowadays
Since the hustlers are gentrifying North Philly's historic ways

F.U.T.U.

This bittersweet relationship has got me loving you one second
Only to remember why I hate you the next
Some of the stunts you pull
Just get me vexed
Like only allowing us to pay tuition with American Express
And charging extra to pay with credit
While most students go into debt it
Makes me enraged how you hustlers do
Having the audacity to call it a convenience fee
Oh yes, it's true

F.U.T.U.

I'm really not one to complain
And don't say this in vain
But damn if there's not a semester
With not understanding my professors
Again, don't mean to be an ass
I understand if it's a language class
But if I had to know English to graduate
They should've too

F.U.T.U.

For paying men more
Housing little whores
Kicking us out of the dorms
For book costs
Community history lost
And triple the frost
For overcrowded classes
Manipulating the masses
Again, kicking us on our asses
For your staff selection
Deadly injection
Even future discretion

F.U.T.U.

I paid twice as much as those from your state
But my home was closer
And double I paid
Have the deans ever seen behind the scenes?
I mean, the basement of Anderson
The SAC's staff stash
All of J&H
Towers and its trash
The lounges that were made for play

Now students live there
So who's getting played?

F.U.T.U.

Just the thought of Health Services makes me sick
No one truly deserves to put up with their shit
Whoever hires these people
Must go to a different doctor
Or never get ill
Because if they sat there for eight hours
Waiting for one pill
I'm sure they will
Excuse me, they would
See what's really good
It's not just the wait
It's so much more
The attitudes I'd get from those whores
I couldn't deal with any day
What made them think I wanted to be there anyway?
Dealing with their problems that they bring to work
That goes for other employees
Who I once wished to hurt

F.U.T.U.

You sometimes get the worst of me
Shafting me for my degree
Would you call it a free ride
If I were doing you?
I already was screwed
So F.U.T.U. too

Poetry is Not a Luxury

I Thought One Poem Would Do It

I thought one poem would do it
I swore it would be the therapy I needed
To get you off my mind
Not you, per "say"
Rather the demons that still haunt me
Yet after all of these years
They will always be here

I thought one poem would do it
But now people still question if it was real
Wondering if the story is mine
Thought I was too specific for you to think I made it up
If you only knew that I only told you because I wish to forget
How I wish to forget
Please, God, help me forget
I'd ask repeatedly before I went to sleep
While I was in the shower
When I walked to school
Lord, help me forget what was done to me

I thought one poem would do it
But now I've learned it's not enough
They still have questions
Wanting to know how scarred I am
Confused about the pain
And why any human would openly share such personal secrets
But they don't understand a poet's mission
I write and recite
They listen and learn
I share my story
And they learn in return
Because I need this cycle to stop repeating itself

I thought one poem would do it
But I know that's a lie
Because the flashbacks keep running through my mind
Time after time
It'll take more than one poem, one line in one rhyme
To make you understand
That when a child is sexually abused
They never will forget
So I never can let you forget
My story
Because for every me
There is a you
And you
And you
And hundreds of thousands more
But people don't like to talk about
what happens behind closed doors
But closed mouths don't help the struggle
I was silent then
But I'll be damned if I don't speak up now
For the you's and me's
Because it is my obligation
As a poet and a woman
Who no longer is a victim
But now a survivor
Of child sexual abuse

I thought one poem would do it
But now I hope you see
That I must continue
To write and recite
While you listen and learn
So I'll share my story
While you learn in return
For the me's and the you's
And those who choose
To keep their silence

Silence is My Enemy

Silence is my enemy
He'll try to shut me up
But no muzzle
Can silence my voice
Not a choice
Just a destiny
As fate would have it
Some were meant to speak
For those who don't
Not because they don't want to
But because they can't

Silence is my enemy
Though he'll never succeed
I like my peace and quiet
But writing is a need
As long as the message is shared
Our people will overcome
But if it's discontinued
Our battle never will be won
That's why he's my nemesis
Closed mouths haven't been fed
Since the genesis
So prepare to harvest the feast

Silence is my enemy
All prophets must agree
Without proper communication
What kind of world would this be?
Silence really would love
For truth to be hidden
But as long as I'm alive
He's got to be kiddin'

Silence is my enemy
But out of respect
Please hold the applause
For a moment of silence

Let it Flow

Not done yet
Can't be finished
Need to keep writing
For those who can't
For those who won't
For those who don't know how
Every word matters
Even if no one hears it
Just because I said so
So I'll write
Nothing can stop me
Just watch and read
And hear me repeat
The need to write
The need to recite
Letting it out
Like a running faucet
Every drop counts
To keep from getting dry
Not keeping dry
It's the other way around
Perhaps better understood by writers
Or readers
Or those into theater
Nonetheless, continue to write
Call it what you will
Titles aren't important, the only thing necessary
Is never to stop
Even if it's a leaky sink
Let it drip
Until you accumulate the drops

Just Because

This is for me, not you
Don't get offended
Didn't mean it like that
Sometimes I just get so caught up
That I need to relax
And take a deep breath
And one step at a time
Write down all that's on my mind
One line at a time
And it's fine
If it doesn't rhyme
Although it'd be nice
But my hand can't catch up
Not even to toast
I don't mean to boast
That's not my style
This is how I express myself
So why not do it with a smile?
Now that I have your undivided attention
I forgot what I was going to say
Already said that this was just for me
But I'll leave you with another one today

Think About It

Some say it hurts to think
The notion is well-debated
But it's done by everyone all day and night
Like an endless cycle of so-called pain – life
That some of us really seem to get off on
But the invisible scars from battle wounds
Don't equally come close to
The knowledge that's consumed
Challenge yourself to think about it
Think about voting
And think about change
Ponder true passion
And question love the same
Think about all of life's "What if's?"
Even the ones that seem far-fetched
Debate Roe vs. Wade to yourself
Think about the state of your mental health
It doesn't hurt until you try it
Really thinking, that is
So if you're brain's in for some pain
I'll leave you with a few things to think about

Only Time Can Tell

Hope this reaches you
Only time can tell the fate
Let the seconds tick

Try again today
As the clock determines awe
Awaiting once more

Could someone tell me?
What do I keep waiting for?
Please let me know now

Play your little game
I can do this all day long
Just you watch me win

Just look at my face
I see what you are doing
End the timeline rhyme

Where Does the Time Go?

Tick, tock
Tick, tock
Tick, tock
Go the hands on my clock
Tick go the seconds
Tock go the minutes
Tick, tock go the hands on my clock
Tick go the hours
Tock go the days
Tick, tock go the hands on my clock
Tick go the weeks
Tock go the months
Tick, tock go the hands on my clock
Tick go the years
Tock goes the time
Tick, tock go the hands of my clock
Tick, tock
Tick, tock
Tick, tock
Tick
Tick
Tick
Stop counting and start living
Or get a new clock
Preferably one that doesn't tick or tock

My Soul's Been Lonely

My soul's been lonely
it needs a friend
Some fulfillment
From deep within

My soul's been tired
for way too long
so sick and tired
of that same song

Something's missing
there's an emptiness
Searching to find it
To relieve the stress

Looking for answers
with open eyes
Better to close them
To mask the disguise

Hollow but warm
Yearning beneath
Old and well-traveled
Justice must seek

My soul's been lonely
it needs a friend
Some fulfillment
From deep within

One and the Same

Connected
On the same levels of comprehension and deepness
No need to try to explain or elaborate my thoughts
You already know
Connected
We are the same, you say
Yet having different genders
In this day and age
Doesn't mean testosterone levels change
Mentality's quick, clever & witty
Hundreds of miles away, but not a pity
Since we're still connected
Someone who finally *gets* me
And shares understanding and knowledge of self
Both no-nonsense go-getters
After the ultimate wealth
Intriguing, enticing, a curious challenge
We are one and the same
Five years with nothing to show
Aside from a few comical memories
You already know
Connected
Even the e-mail names
Different languages, but one and the same
So it's a shame
Communications aren't increased
Though no love lost
When you come back east
You already know
Connected
One and the same

Close Strangers

How do you know me?
We just met
Still, you understand me more than the woman who
birthed me decades ago
And so, I wonder what it is
That unified our spirits
Perhaps a past connection
From a previous life
Maybe we marched together
Through the suffering and strife
Or we could just as easily
Be so different ourselves
That we 'get' each other's deepness
I knew you were reaching out
Before you picked up the phone
It's refreshing to have this feeling
Like my spirit's not alone
And just maybe you're the real reason
Behind all five of those poems
Most would think we're crazy
They just don't understand
Sometimes that's how we like it
Call me a believer, but don't title my faith
Surprised you have that label
Are you just playing it safe?
Regardless, there's just so much to share
That I'm not sure where to begin
My spirit's just satisfied
That it found a friend

Like a Simile

I want this to get under your skin
Like a splinter
Since you got my heart feelin' cold
Like the winter
Now the absence of my presence
Will unconsciously sting you like acid rain
And you'd wish you'd be down with S&M
Like, "Pass the pain!"
Now I'll keep it quiet
Like "Shhh! My mom's right across the hall."
No need to be shook
Like fright of a boss' call
You'll come first
Like first comes last
And I'll haunt you
Like the Ghost of Christmas Past
There's no three guesses
Like there's no Kazaam
And I ain't yah girl
Like you ain't my man
But this is a confusing coincidence
Like insurance covering abortion
But not birth control pills
Reality is a distortion
Like requiem thrills
You left me here
Like I wasn't even last pick
I just got placed on the team
I was abandoned
Like a motherless baby
Who couldn't help but scream
You can't just flush this away
Like excrement or bile
And yes I get impatient
Like, "This is taking a while"

But I still smile
Like a façade over sorrow
Because deep down I know
There'll be a better tomorrow

I Had a Dream

I wanna live, but not by myself
I wanna be rich, but I'm not talking about wealth
I wanna be strong, but regardless of my health
I wanna teach, but not by speaking
I wanna look, but without seeking
I wanna learn, but not because you said so
I wanna hold on, but I wanna let go
I wanna cry, but not out of fear
I wanna love, but you're not near
I wanna sing, but there's no one to hear
I wanna preach, but not if you don't learn
I wanna speak, but it's not my turn
I wanna have power, but not through violence
I wanna have quiet, but not silence
I wanna be heard, but not my screaming
I wanna be seen, but not by scheming
I wanna dream, but I'm just dreaming

Emptiness

Empty
I feel empty
Like a broke man's wallet
Or an anorexic girl's stomach
Like trash bins on Friday mornings
Or paychecks after taxes
Just empty
Something is missing
It's just not there
I don't know what it is
But it has me feeling bare...blank, vacant, unfilled...empty
Seeing the glass as half full is an exaggeration
Focusing on the empty is supposed to be pessimistic
But I don't know what could fill the other half
I need to quench my thirst
Instead of cups I need glasses
To see what I'm searching for
Don't say it's been hiding in front of me the whole time
Don't tell me it's Jesus
Or another man
And don't think a vacation could fill this void

Emptiness
It's what I feel when I'm intimate
When I go to sleep
When I'm at work
I want to feel life
I want to fee like I'm not acting life
I want to feel something other than anger
(Which I feel entirely too frequently)
The anger leaves me feeling even emptier
Wondering where the true happiness is
Knowing things don't have to be this way
But not understanding why they are
And why I'm so alone in this big city

Wondering where to go to next
Too busy focusing on the next step
So time flies yet emptiness is there
Staring me in the face every time I look in the mirror
And see my reflection
This daily routine that pays my bills
Buys my meals, but avoids the thrills
Leaving me so submissive that I'm often convinced I'm powerless
But knowing damn well I should be running this
instead of running

So, if a poem can change the world
Than perhaps it can and will
Do so, one person at a time
Starting here
Starting now
With me
Filling this emptiness
To allow me to provide you poetry for the soul
Soul-filled
Fulfilled
Tag – you're it
How will you change the world?

Love vs. Lust

Crush Trilogy

I. Passion's Poison

I'm in a race to write
Because our eyes kissed
And I don't wanna fake the fight
With passion and bliss
Let our words make love
I want your first language to be my last name
And have your seeds flowing through my veins
Damn, could you imagine how beautiful they'd be?
See, I must be trippin' because you just met me

Okay, I know women like to speed things up
But this seems so right that it's left
Left to the passion that'd drive my thoughts crazy enough to
jump...
...outta my pen and onto paper
While I'm driving on I95 during rush hour
And the only collision I'm thinking about is
You bumping into me
No seatbelt or airbag can save me now

Picasso's paintings and Neruda's words
Don't compare to your mother's creation
When smiles become contagious it hurts
Knowing we have to be patient
Though I can't help but think that it's fate
Causing us to send the same messages simultaneously
Our passion doesn't require a scientist
To figure out this chemistry
Or is it simply the curiosity
Of what it could be?
Could be or should be?
Or what it would be?
I can't help but wonder

Perhaps it's the mesmerizing exotic passion
That's poising my thoughts and actions

You see, while we've been having this emotional affair
My man's been faithful
And your girl's still there
That's why I'll remain wondering
Instead of wandering
Pondering passion's poison

II. Thinking of You…As Usual

I can't get you off my mind.
It's like the same old tune
That I can't get enough of
An addiction, infatuation, obsession
Call it what you will,
But my mind can't stop focusing on you
Your universe, existence and entire being
My subconscious and cognizant are aligned
And the only thing I think about more than you
Is how I can get you off my mind
And why you're even there in the first place
I can't seem to put my finger on it
Perhaps that's why my imagination races…
If you know what I mean.
I find myself wanting to send you messages –
Electronically, physically, spiritually
But I'm on the other end wondering
"Can you hear me now?"
I think about you so much that my thoughts
don't allow my pen to catch-up
Therefore the images in my mind have me drawing blanks
When daydreams + wet dreams = fantasies
My mind and eyes can fantasize
Cuz my hands are too busy writing
Writing…riding…however it is that poets seem to get off
Get off…get off…get off my mind!
A fix is for addicts
So I know that won't do for me
Though seemingly stressing
It's not obsession
C….K is not my scent
Could be infatuation or frustration
But at this point, labels aren't important
I can't give a title to something that isn't mine
Can I?

Can I call you my "mental stimulation" without explanation?
Or "my poetry" and just let it be?
See, my mind continues on in these meaningless circles of rambles
That you'll never hear
Well, I suppose you could,
but that would just take all of the fun out of it
Now wouldn't it?
Think about it.

III. The Aftermath

One night
Two people
One bed
Two drinks
One chance
Two options
One word
NO!

Adding me equals three
And I prefer it even
Subtract the third
Or forget multiplying
According to my calculator,
You should've pressed "clear" a long time ago
Who'd want to divide for a fraction?
Besides, I've got the bigger half
I already hit equal
Now you do the math

One night
Two people
One bed
Two drinks
One chance
Two options
One word
NO!

Before & After

I. Worth the Wait

Last night, she kissed my soul
Then our eyes made love
Passion electrified sparks conducted through veins
Because it was from the heart
I wanted to consume her spirit
Since touch is only tangible
And her energy is greater than her physical being
I never thought I'd feel this way again
She's the missing piece that I just couldn't seem to find
But had been hiding in front of me the whole damn time
Her happiness is my satisfaction
So naturally her smile leads to action
And only a fraction of friction
Heats the sexual diction
That arouses the aura and connection
No other woman could compete
At making me feel complete
Well, at least that's what he told me

II. *Worthless*

You aren't worth a second of my time
Nor a penny or dime
Of my finances
The circumstances
Lead me to believe that you aren't
Worth a drop of my tears
Even after all these years
You're just worthless

You aren't worth an ounce of my energy
Or second of my memory
Not worth a free text message, night & weekend minute or e-mail
Only thing you're good for is nothing
Worth + nothing = worthless
Making you, worthless

You aren't worth a stroke of my pen
Or a joke to a friend
Not another day, let alone decade
You aren't even worth meeting in a past life
That's how worthless you are

Worthless enough to not know these feelings, these words exist
So unless you pay to hear me recite them
I'll save my breath
Cuz you're not even worth knowing
How worthless you are

Special Delivery

Hey!
I'm here
Can't you see me?
I'm waving
Waving my love in front of your face
Like a red flag in front of a bull
But this bull thinks this is bull...shit,
Did I go off again, my friend?
Your friend – that's me
Your "homie"
But you are not my friend
You are the tip of Cupid's evil arrow that dove through my aorta
And ripping you out will hurt twice as much as your entrance
Because you exit
And dream there while you sleep here
Eat here while you hunger there
Like I can quench your undying thirst
But I'm not the right flavor
But savor your savior
So you can save me for later
But I am no leftover
I am not take-out
I am home-cooked
Like you don't have to scrape the plate
Like "That meal was great!"
Like dessert can wait
Cuz I just wanna let this taste
This feeling
Marinate and linger
Like sucking your fingers
To receive your tongue's orgasmic state
Were you maced?
Since you can only temporarily see that
Like you temporarily see me
Our transient transactions of compassion

Lead to my bittersweet reactions
I need satisfaction
But our chances are like "rock, paper, scissors....SHIT"
I went off again
Sorry, dear "friend"
But I'm just torn in two
As I'm turned into
Trains of translucent tragedies
Since half of me sees through you
But you're still here
Well.....there
Torn like the seams of the jeans
You know you had no business trying on
Crying long
Before they truly rip
Just damaged
Though something's held them together
Torn like the weather
On the days when the sun can't seem to decide
Whether it wants to shine or hide
Torn like my insides
Fighting love with hate
Contemplating the severity of confusion
Illusioned by your reality
As much as I hate to see you leave
I love to watch you go
So grow, build, be filled with this
Before I piss on this notion of devotion
And least but not last
I ask that you don't live for the past
Because your future no longer is present

School Me

We did it. We finally did it.
Our minds and bodies made economics
When we reached equilibrium
As supply and demand weren't the only things that went up
The quantity curve then shifted and uplifted
Leading us to do it
Leading us to make psychology
Cuz I was stuck in the genital stage
And couldn't repress any denial
When he saw my smile
Even a straight jacket couldn't restrain me
From going crazy
Far from lazy
So no need for a shrink
We made finance, so the hell with getting paid
I just found where I'm socially secure
And we can't ignore that I made foreign languages by myself
Cuz I was saying things that neither of us could translate
Or even pronounce
But I will announce that he can roll R's with that tongue
Shoot, he could probably roll L's with that tongue
But anyways, he passed my night school with straight A's
And with praise, we made religion (Hallelujah)
But a specific division
More like death and dying
Cuz I killed it after he dug six feet deep
But he wasn't even trying to go to sleep
Best believe we made math
Because when you add both halves
And subtract clothes
Divide legs and multiply multiples
That equals "Aaaah" to the 7th power
And every hour
Its African-American studies cross-listed with anatomy
But it had to be chemistry

That sparked my mere curiosity
We each played a role without acting
So we skipped theater
Maybe next time when there's a bigger stage
But I turned the page
To continue making history
The ending's not a mystery
It'll end blissfully
Just like the start
When we majored in the arts
Sculpting our bodies no further apart
Dancing to music, building crescendos as mere innuendos
That we didn't wanna let go
Of this harmonious rapture
That we seemed to capture
Paint, mold and make
As visionary as a utopian landscape
He schooled me
Now I know why kinesiology is his field
All my muscles went through massage therapy
And were healed
The touch of energy lead to reflexes
Unlike that of any ex's
We made detention – cuz he held me long after
Might I mention, I didn't think to watch the clock
Counting each tick and dreading each tock
It wasn't punishment cuz after he went, we both got our work done
Then he gazed at me
We did it. We finally did it. We made poetry.

What It Is?

Tell me how you feel.

Tell me you wanna cook for me, feed me, and then be my dessert
just so you could digest my spirit to feed your soul

Tell me you wanna kiss me from head to toe,
then to head while looking at my face

Tell me you wanna meet my parents to thank them for creating me
Because God's heard it too many times already

Tell me I'm the prototype, the kind you like,
despite the fear of reality's bite cuz you know it's right

So tell me I make you wanna sing
 – not like blues or country or pop,
but like Mary belting to hip-hop
Ella scattin', Mariah screachin'
Or Marvin reaching…sexual healing
Tell me what you're feeling

Or you could tell me I make you excited
Excited enough to bust
Over just the thought of lust
Because U & I make the "us" in trust
So there's no limit when you're up in it

Tell me you wanna be my cell phone
Never on roam
Just so you're the first thing I wake up to
Then carry around all day
Only to fall asleep next to each and every night

Tell me I'm your favorite food because every bite
Your tongue touches
Your taste buds have orgasms
That pregnant cravings couldn't fathom

Tell me I'm your contacts cuz you see right through me
And read through visions of me to help you see clearly

Tell me my mulligrubs are bagatelle to you
Because either way you're turned on
And with exclusive adit
My love makes you feel volitant
So take flight off palisades
And land in the Armenian ocean
Where life is made

Tell me you wanna be my mirror
So you'd know the real me
The one whom I see
I'd sing and dance for you
And no one else
Door locked
Captured audience
Reflective criticism

Tell me I would be your Juliet
But this is far from a tragedy
But if we act like play
I'll put the "O" after brav
When we make lav
Not love
Because this shit deserves an "A"
And if I could take the plus from Pert
I'd do it since we make the best two-in-one work

Tell me you wanna be my blanket
So you can wrap around me
Providing comfort & warmth
From dusk till dawn
Touching me everywhere simultaneously
While I submerge in your existence

Tell me you love me
I know actions speak louder than words
But damn
Just tell me how you wanna take me somewhere
exotic, romantic & private without leaving your crib
Then sleep inside me
To wake up on the right side of the bed
The next morning

Tell me you wanna write a poem
Just like this one
Actually, tell me how you feel
Since I just told you.

Valentine's Day

February 14
No calls
No cards
No candles
Nothing

No flowers
No chocolates
No jewelry
Nothing

No e-mails
No dinner reservations
And certainly no sex

This was my Valentine's Day
Needless to say
This is why I said, "Next!"

Thanks for the wake up call
And discarding my affection
You let the flame die
Though I placed the rejection

Our love wilted
Liked the flowers I should've received would've done too
Sweets couldn't compare
To all I've done for you
Nor the rock foundation
I'm so through with you

Done sending messages
And wasting my time
Physical pleasure doesn't measure
But I'll be just fine
I'll be damned if I wait until next year
To find a new valentine

2:40

Break-Ups are Easier Done Than Said

Antidisestablishmentarianism.
A-N-T-I
Anti.
The prefix in opposition
A counteractive mission
Going against the grain
Hostile toward the same
D-I-S
Dis.
Opposite & deprived
Exclude, apart
Prefix meaning not
So it's used toward the start
E-S-T-A-B-L-I-S-H
Establish.
To institute permanently
To make firm or stable
Or to be able
To gain acceptance or recognition
In other words to prove
M-E-N-T
Ment.
A set stage, place or action
A condition or process
Object or result like satisfaction
A-R-I-A-N
Arian.
Advocate, believer
Producer, conceiver
I-S-M

Ism.
Condition, act or process

Theory, doctrine or practice
No need for an actress
Because this cause
Is the state of being
Antidisestablishmentarianism.
Against the opposition of the stable condition
believed to be practiced

Say What?

Not having the words to say
Is like not knowing your origins
Born an illiterate orphan
Adopted by a dictionary
Scrambling for words like Pictionary
Frustration's like non-fiction – scary

If I knew the words
To change the world
I'd recite them for every ear
I'd make everyone listen
As opposed to hear

If I knew the words
I did not have
I'd write them down
Then shout them out
I'd turn tears to stream down faces
I'd unite hands of all supposed races
I'd scream so loud I couldn't be shushed
I'd make gay men hard enough to fuck George's bush

If I knew the words
I did not have
I wouldn't really need 'em
To know 'em is to have them
And to have them is to love them
I guess that's all I have to say

Demons

My stepbrother put his hands on me.
I was too young to play his game
The shame – has guilted me
From tongue to dick to pick-up sticks
My body has been violated
I can shower until my skin is pruned
But the dirt and filth my honor's consumed
I'd never wish my nemesis to live with
Lost searching solo for justice
Why must this
Struggle continue so slow?
So go and grow with what you know

My stepbrother put his hands on me.
They were over twice the size of mine
At that time
He was over double my age
So rage
Now fills my heart
Tears it apart
Playing house at age six
Shouldn't consist of sex
The invest on incest
Was enough to make one hurl
The foreign objects in my vagina
Would make your toes curl
He said he was "playing the organ"
But church was far away
My mother was in the next room
But was lead astray

My stepbrother put his hands on me.
But he wasn't the only one
Some guy from church would do it upstairs
And called it "having fun"

They never hit me or called me names
But I was a baby
And they were insane
Still no one noticed
No one believed
No one noticed
No one believed
No one noticed
No one believed

My stepbrother put his hands on me
Day or night alike
Because he lived downstairs and came right up
When they turned off the lights
No monster scared me more
Than this Boogey Man
With wandering hands
That rubbed me while asleep
I was terrified
So I lied
Underneath my sheets

My stepbrother put his hands on me
And now he walks the streets
Mom didn't care
No one was there
How fast my heart still beats
When I think of the past
How long will this last?
Wishing for justice
But just this time
I'll be fine
It's the youth I now worry about

My stepbrother put his hands on me
No one noticed
No one believed

No one noticed
No one believed
Notice!
Believe!

Times Like This

[Chorus]
Life always births me times like this
When solitude breaches confinement
And desire disguises bliss
When hugs feel too empty
Sometimes it takes a kiss
(Oh, times like this)

Even my dreams remind me
...there are times like this
Don't wanna look behind the
...times been missed
Repression neutralizes depression
Just to keep you sane
Cuz insanity flows like blood cells
Through each of your veins
During times like this

[Chorus]
Life always births me times like this
When solitude breaches confinement
And desire disguises bliss
When hugs feel too empty
Sometimes it takes a kiss
(Oh, times like this)

Times like this I just wanna run free
Rip through my clothes & start a family
Tell one to fuck two cuz I love three
Then cop more rings than an ancient tree
Just so you could be jealous of my fingers
And so the envy lingers

I'll stick one up, just for you
Actually, never mind let's make that two
Only when there are times like this

[Chorus]
Life always births me times like this
When solitude breaches confinement
And desire disguises bliss
When hugs feel too empty
Sometimes it takes a kiss
(Oh, times like this)

Take Flight

Living with limits
Dying with dictation
Counting the minutes
Destruction of the nation

Fighting the battle
To win the war
Herded like cattle
Justice is sore

Why must this be?
Resistant restriction
I want to be free
Tell me its fiction

Awareness awaken & ignorance die
Till then we'll remain asking "Why?"

Epitaph

Here lies Meredith Zabelle Avakian a.k.a. MZA b.k.a. Miz
An Armenian Queen
Born to do great things
May she be remembered
In our hearts, spirits & minds
All of the time
Do not forget her passion for justice
And love for poetry
May God bless her soul
While she rests in peace

Printed in the United States
205201BV00001B/406-666/P

9 781438 908328